MW01602805

SUMMARY

of

The Plant Paradox

The Hidden Dangers in Healthy Foods
That Cause Disease and Weight Gain

STEVEN R. GUNDRY M.D

InstantReads

ISBN-13: 978-1-948191-56-2
ISBN-10: 1-948191-56-3

Disclaimer/ Terms of Use

TABLE OF CONTENT

Key Takeaways

Review And Analysis Of Plant Paradox

Ultimate List of Lectin Free Foods To Replace For Healthy Weight Loss

Introduction

This book is for anyone who can't take control of their raging appetite or cravings for certain foods. Several diets such as Paleo, low-glycemic, low- carb, low-fat, and so many other diets have been created with different recipes and meal plans yet, they haven't helped. Rather they have turned out to be intolerable and unsustainable such that after the initial success of losing some weight, the lost weight quickly crept back making the weight loss journey a total waste of time. On the other hand, carrying out exercise trainings such as high-intensity interval training, aerobics, core training, weight training, yoga, running, speed walking, CrossFit, spinning, or whichever exercise program(s) many have embarked upon has not helped in banishing the stubborn extra pounds rather it has actually increased the cravings for food.

Your primary concern might be weight control or the various unexplainable signs you experience at different times of the day. It could be allergies or even so many diseases that are autoimmune related. Well, this program will be your last stop as all of that is about to change. You are about to be repaired and restored back to the right body weight, lifestyle and increased life span.

Within this book, Dr Gundry examined in a gradual way the various reasons why over the decades, man has gotten worse despite the advent of recipes and diet plans which seem to work. He collated his research of many years to present a workable procedure that would move you from your current state to a better one and also maintain it.

In as much as the harm has been done, Dr Gundry assures you that your current body state can be reversed to the normal way it is meant to be. Away from the norm which is flooding the internet towards the right path which makes more sense with achievable results.

Using his wealth of knowledge, extensive research, years of practice and personal experience Dr Gundry shows an achievable path in the journey towards achieving a better state of health. This he further reinstated as a fact giving reason that even the heart can be fixed without surgery.

Having written a book on Diet Evolution which elaborated the effects diet has on the human genes with respect to diseases that have destroyed the body; he was propelled towards a better outlook on treating diseases of the body with food, this time, the right way.

He explains that the immune system can be fooled to accept anything having literally studied and analyzed the different the effect of food and its availability within the body. He was able to define particularly that most people who had bodily issues are the causative agents as they brought it upon themselves due to the war between themselves and their body. He also attributed the effects noticed to the different over-the-counter and self medications we ingest which damage the normal flora in the gut.

The basic principle obtained in this book is simply the application of well thought out working strategies that are made up of vegetables, limited amounts of high-quality protein sources, as well as certain fruits (but only in season), tree nuts, and certain dairy products and oils. Foods omitted were ones that come from commonly accepted ingredients such as these vegetables; tomatoes, peppers and their related ones.

Thus:

PART 1 provides a general summary of the root causes of these diseases and its mechanism of affecting the body

PART 2 contains information on how to start off the program with the help of a three-day cleanse which will facilitate your body to heal your damaged gut, feed and grow your microbial gut with the right foods

PART 3 is a step into the program itself after you have cleansed your body from the unwanted. He explains how to achieve your desired health state as well as to maintain it to ensure you experience longetivity.

CHAPTER 1: The War Between Plants and Animals

Key Takeaways:

- Plants create toxins which we readily eat in "healthy foods"

- To survive and continue existence, plants create master plans against predators

- The plants you enjoy are edible enemies that produce lectins which disrupt your body function

- Your health depends on what passes through your mouth

A detailed description of the reasons behind the effectiveness of certain diets is presented by Dr Gundry. He describes the ultimate reason why plants cause diseases and illness based on researches and previous studies carried out by different scientists.

He based his facts on the need for survival. These plants just like everything living had the tendency and scientific injunction to grow reproduce and continue their existence. In order to achieve this, he claims they had to continuously evolve and mutate to protect themselves. These mutations he believed led to the production of poisonous, harmful or even healing plants as they are now as the increase in their destruction increased.

In order to survive in the midst of its predators, Dr Gundry explained that these plants evolved to a stage where they produced toxins known as lectin which are targeted against their predators-mammals and insects. He provided a descriptive explanation on the effects long term consumption of these harmful foods had on the body. They may have little or no effect at the moment but he assured when they do they would be fully blown with very devastating effects observed.

In further statements, using the color differences when plants are due for consumption and when not right, Dr Gundry gave a clear picture on how the seeds of plants either naked or covered increases the body's state of ill health all year long. He claims this is one of the strategies plants use in destroying the body system of its predators. Writing on the types of fruits plants produce; he drew attention to the different types of toxins released by the consumption of various diets that were believed to work. He went ahead to state the implications of prolonged consumption of fruits that were artificially ripened that is to say prevented from getting naturally ripened. Citing typical examples on case studies of patients and researches already done, he was able to shed more light on the truth behind these organisms wanting to survive in the face of predation.

In summary, he reinstated that the paradox of plant is based on the need to treat the plants according to the types of seeds, use them when needed and to cook them in the right way. Also, he advocates the need to redirect into a whole new world of animal sea food as they contained proteins essential for your survival with little or no toxins to look out for.

CHAPTER 2: Lectins on the Loose

Key Takeaways

- The evolving man is yet to be in pace with the evolving plants

- Changes in the gut has made lectins to have more damaging effects on the body system

- Our conception of healthy food is based on the influence of our genetic makeup.

- The myths we have on the right foods are wrong and grains are the determining factor of our health state

- The most deadly lectins are not the gluten but wheat germ agglutinin (WGA).

The advent of cooking plants properly before cooking was used by Dr Gundry as basis to explain why the guts of the ancient species were able to survive the toxic effect of lectins, the toxins used in self defense against the body. Cooking, as he psited, took up the work of the guts allowing its function of breakdown of lectins to be diminished to the barest minimum. However, with reference to the changes in evolution of man, Gundry stated that the gut has become exposed to entirely new lectins which are yet to be be understood by the body during digestion. Providing a classification of plant predators, Gundry explained further to show that humans who are tree dwellers and processed the lectins in two-leaf plants were yet to evolve to have similar gut metabolic activity as the lower species of mammalian plant predators that digested the lectins in single-leaf plants. This setback he argued is the real reason behind the current dietary dilemma humans are in.

Giving evidence from research and current trends in plant studies, he clearly presented that these plants are evolving faster than humans. He assumed this was causing a winning drift towards the part of the plants in the war of surviving. He gave reasons for this assumptions to be as a result of increased disruption of the normal flora by lectins as seen in the different diseases whose statistics are constantly arising as the day goes by.

Proposing different cataclysmic changes in the human diet, he explained how these lectins which were on the loose brought about their destructive effect on the human body. These epic changes are:

CHANGE 1: The Agricultural Revolution

He defined this as change into the consumption of more grains and legumes and less of animal fat, tubers, proteins and leaves basically. The change he said was due to the need to survive as soon as the last Ice Age ended.

CHANGE 2: A Mutation in Cow

He stated records of cows which mutated to change from release of normal casein A-2 to protein casein A-1 in their milk. The new form of protein on digestion causes the release of lectin-like protein that exhibits the effects of lectin within your body. To this effect, he recommended the use of A-2 dairy products or use of goat or sheep milk.

CHANGE 3: Plants from the New World

He also brought to light the impact foods from the New World had on the gut and the entire unprepared system. These foods he mentioned were still related to grains, legumes, chia and other seeds.

CHANGE 4: Contemporary Innovations

This change was seen to be drawn from the negative improvements of organic foods which made the lectins to be unleashed in a higher frequency than it was in the unprocessed form. Therefore, With these postulates, he went ahead to negate and declare the Standard American Diet as unhealthy and gave the right type of food as one with lectin-rich food and more of animal rich foods.

With research and facts garnered over the years, Gundry uncovered how lectins are infiltrating our bodies through plant based recipes and diets.

CHAPTER 3: Your Gut Under Attack

Key Takeaways

- Your gut is the main route that determines the level of your health

- Lectins are large proteins that should normally not pass through the gut but with drugs

- Drugs especially NSAID's are the disruptors of the immune system paving way for lectins to penetrate into the body

- The real cause of Autoimmune diseases are the foods you call healthy which destroy the gut

Giving scientific descriptions and findings, Dr Gundry provided a better understanding as to how the gut functions in the presence and absence of lectins. He stated that the gut was part of the body's own defensive mechanism from harmful substances such as the lectins and other microbes that seek to penetrate and harm the body. He gave the different types of disruptors that affected the gut in addition to their various effects after a long while. Starting off with an explanation of the mutual relationship micro organisms had with their human as host, he created a correlation on health and weight issues. He further explained that the relationship humans had with this holobiome, a name depicting a collection of these bacteria, started from the maternal birth canal of every child born. This holobiome he believed were in the gut which is supposedly expected to prevent the passage of lectins and at the same time, make sure these microbes remain where they are meant to be-outside the intestines. With this, he concluded on the need for good gut health as they only can make nutrients to pass through only in smaller forms obtained from food digestions.

Citing samples of different cases, Dr Gundry explained the effects the use of excessive analgesics and pain relieving medications had on the intestine such as leaky gut syndrome. He advocates that the health state becomes worse if grains or foods containing transglutaminase are consumed along with plant based recipes. According to various articles, he said that they rather make the GI to become more porous and open.

Using the cases of different patients he had treated, Gundry postulated that the real cause of the so many auto immune diseases the body experiences are all related to a leaky gut, which he defines as a change in the permeability of the gut wall and mouth and gums. He added that the only way to repair the gut which had been damaged from the effects of lectins was to stop eating lectins that is foods that are rich in them or could release them. Repairing the gut as he recommended was important to ensure the good health of the gut and at the same time, allowing the gut microbes get the required nutrients they need to survive.

CHAPTER 4: Know Thy Enemy: The Seven Deadly Disruptors

Key Takeaways

- Foods we eat do not heal, they hasten our death

- Abuse of Broad-Spectrum Antibiotics and analgesics(NSAIDS) reduces longevity as it kills the microbes in the gut

- The stomach acids should be allowed to do the work they are meant for.

- Sweeteners and preservatives that disrupt the endocrine mimic the natural hormones kick starting fat accumulation and weight gain

- Organic forms of food nourish the microbes in the gut

- Too much exposure to blue light increases our risks of gaining more weight

Gundry discussed on the various disruptors that pave way for lectins to seep through the gut easily. He made clear in various cited examples from patient success stories, the impact these disruptors had been causing which are way beyond the diseases they cause

He argued with well researched facts how the state of health had deteriorated rather than being better despite the acclaimed belief that health matters had become fair. In a further statement, he provided with startling evidence the damages that were occurring within the body as a result of the poor diet regimen being used which the body had completely adjusted to.

Having declared the various effects and long term damages these disruptors had created, he listed the seven types of disruptors

DISRUPTOR 1: Broad-Spectrum Antibiotics

He showed with statistical data how the continuous use of antibiotics predisposed its users to lectin effects. He explained further that the use of the antibiotics could be direct when abused or indirect when used in fattening chickens and cows.

DISRUPTOR 2: Nonsteroidal Anti-Inflammatory Drugs (NSAIDs)

Using his wealth of knowledge on the effects of long term use of NSAID as a medical practitioner, Gundry elucidated on the damaging effects these analgesics had on the gut flora.

DISRUPTOR 3: Stomach-Acid Blockers

This type of disruptor he believed caused kidney disease in the long run as it helps to allow the normal flora to move out of their designated homes and this can lead to gut barrier disruption, creating protein over filled individuals and the occurrence of diseases. Having explained the impact of these disruptors on the health of the gut, he conclude that it is of importance that stomach acid be allowed to serve its bodily function which implies reducing or stopping the use of stomach-acid blockers.

DISRUPTOR 4: Artificial Sweeteners

Gundry stated the effects this disruptor contributed to the consumer such as increased weight gain, reduction in the micro flora, disruption of the internal body clock and advocated they are removed entirely as they were unhealthy causing more harm than good.

DISRUPTOR 5: Endocrine Disruptors

Gundry described these disruptors as preservatives found in various food/edible forms that not only deplete certain vitamins in the body but also destroy the same microbial flora required to prevent lectin permeability. Also, he brought to light how these disruptors could mimic that of the normal body hormones giving rise to the body's similar outburst for fat consumption and deposition.

DISRUPTOR 6: Genetically Modified Foods and the Herbicide Roundup

This type of disruptors, he claimed came from genetic modification of foods either by the industrial production or use of insecticides or pesticides on the plant. According to the different test results he had obtained from his patients, he declared that these damages caused by the disruptors were correlated such that using herbicides ends up assisting genetically modified foods to give a disease state

DISRUPTOR 7: Constant Exposure to Blue Light

He recommends reduced exposure to sunlight, which he called blue light. Reason because research has shown that sunlight tends to keep the body in a state of summer which is perceived by the body's circadian rhythm as the time to accumulate pounds. Presently, we are always exposed to blue light which dominates our modern life. This way of life creates, unnaturally and practically exposes nonstop us to this wavelength. Cell phones, televisions, tablets, games, laptops and other electronic devices, and even certain types of energy-saving lightbulbs are capable of emitting light which are found in the blue range of the spectrum. This part of the spectrum is known to interfere with sleep as it suppresses the production of melatonin, the body's circadian clock that helps one to fall asleep. This blue light also stimulates ghrelin and cortisol, which are, respectively, the "hunger" and "awake" hormones. Given that we are genetically programmed to associates blue light with daylight, being constantly exposed tends to trick our bodies into thinking we're perpetually in the summer, a season with longer daylight hours. This starts of the endocrine hormones to pack on pounds in anticipation of the shorter daylight hours of upcoming winter, which however would never arrive due to these electric lights. With the disruption of our body's ancient rhythm, the body lives in 365 days of "endless summer."

Finally, please don't be misled when you come to poultry. The organic, free-range label does not explain that these birds were kept in a warehouse (they do not have access to the outdoors) and they were not fed organic corn and soybeans. It is advised that you put down the package when you see "fed an all vegetarian diet," and quietly step away from the meat counter. Truth is, chickens are insectivores, not grain eaters. Also, if a fish label says it is organic Scottish, Norwegian, or Canadian salmon, put it right back. These statements all mean that the fishes were fed organic grains and soybeans. Don't think they really followed the salmon around to see if they were eating "organic" seaweed? The same applies to organic beef—if the label does not also specify that the animal was grass-fed and grass-finished, suspect a trick. All cows at some point in their life must eat grass.

Therefore, whether in theory and in practice, all beef can be—and is—labeled grass-fed, in as much as the cow spent most of its life eating grains and beans in a feedlot. The damage our body has sustained from eating lectins makes it all the more vulnerable to the additional assaults caused by these disruptors. When lectins and LPSs destroy and breach the intestine's containment walls, your body enter into a defensive state. In order to have sufficient calories to fuel the white blood cells (the immune system's army) fighting the war within the body, the muscles are genetically engineered to become insulin- and leptin-resistant. The human body is created to be insulin-resistant and leptin-resistant (a term denoted as metabolic syndrome) not because we're fat. We become fat due to teh storage of calories from the signal sent for the war effort.

CHAPTER 5: How the Modern Diet Makes You Fat (and Sick)

Key Takeaways

- Western diet, the environment, and inactivity for our poor health and excess pounds are not the primary cause of our health crisis

- "Diets" are among the myths that have distracted us from the real issues regarding our health.

- An integral part of self-healing is achieving the weight your body "wants" to be and not what you want it to be

- Exercise doesn't help you lose weight

- Grains and beans are fast ways of fattening up but also fast killers

Dr Gundry makes clear his beliefs and notions on the effect of food in treatment of diseases and maintenance of a true healthy body. He commented on how the assumed Standard American Diet makes people fat rather than healthy as expected. With three simple key points to be noted, he explained the relationship between the modern diet and the gut flora. These three points are:

-the wrong foods which are causing more harm than good

-the importance of the gut flora and

-the relationship between disease and weight issues

The author criticized the Western diet stating that along with inactivity and the environment that they were the true causes of the decrease in the current state of health as it has been discovered to cause a deterioration in the human physique and structure. He argued that with most diets and different types of exercise training, the diseased human body will not heal as the real reason behind the actual fat accumulation is yet to be removed from meals. He however affirmed that exercises can only maintain weight with other benefits but not to help with loss of weight nor bring about the much needed good health.

Drawing the reader to refer back to ancient times when food was scarce, Gundry opined that weight gain from consuming the lectins in grains and beans was a huge benefit at that time, but today, the same result works against the body as our healthy microbes have been damaged by plant based diets and medications. He explains further that weight gain arises from the body's defensive mechanism of storing more fat in the event of a rise in inflammation caused by lectin containing foods

Analyzing other diets which has been trending, Gundry commented that these diets worked at first due to:

-the initial removal of lectin containing foods

-elimination of fats

-use of whole unprocessed grains and

-use of organic grains

He however claims that they failed on the long run due to either being intolerable or that their maintenance phase caused re-introduction of lectins. The latter statement he supported with stating that the human genes accepts diets that makes one to eat more animal protein and less carbs in order to reproduce and get out of the way for its offspring to survive. He suggests that eating certain carbs with no lectins or with lectins with which the body microbes have been familiar with for millennia are okay. This could only be if there can be minimization of certain animal proteins. He goes ahead to claim that it can reduce the aging process and in turn give more energy. Using Kitavans as an example, he stated that there are carbs that are not carbs because of its content and friendliness to microbes adding that plant leaves can give rise to high fat diets as these all feed the gut bacteria rather than deplete its ability to do its work as "healthy foods" do.

CHAPTER 6: Revamp Your Habits

Key Takeaways

- Your good health is affected by what you stopped eating

- Feed the gut and it will give you a longer lifespan

- Fruits are sweet killers

- If you must eat lectins, kill them with proper cooking

- Diets based on lots of animal protein make your body worse

Gundry discussed the four rules required to help in achieving a successful Plant Paradox program:

-what one needs to stop eating is more important than what one starts to eat.

He insisted that one ultimately has to watch the intake of animal protein and to use fish as source of animal protein, to ensure no calorie counting and also to indulge in less of food which serves as entry points for lectins such as chicken sandwich that introduces corn into the body. These listed foods he maintained caused osteopenia and osteoporosis in chickens and would transfer the same to humans.

-Paying attention to the care and feeding of the gut bugs as they will in turn handle the care and feeding of the human body through directing the appetite and management of cravings. The cravings other diets caused he claimed came from eating high protein foods which gets digested as fat to become carriers of lectins that inflame the brain sparking off hunger.

-Fruit Might as Well Be Candy

He criticizes the notion that the consumption of fruit is healthy. Explaining this criticism, he related back to his earlier stated fact that the seeds of fruit still contain lectins which he recommends to be avoided in entirety.

-You Are What the Thing You Are Eating, Ate

Gundry stated that the current health state one has, is based on the content of what one was eating.

With the four recommended rules for the program stated, Gundry gave the importance of the program, stating that the difference between plant paradox and other diets programs was on the ability to achieve a reduction in food cravings. Gundry also believed that even vegetarians who eat the wrong plants can also exploit and benefit from the diet regimen if they would use an automatic pressure cooker for their meals. This method from patient success stories affirmed his recommendations in a thorough destruction of these lectins.

Gundry recommended a single 3-ounce serving a day as the right amount of protein to consume based on one's lean body mass to prevent accumulation of protein as a result of continuous consumption of over-proteinized American diet.

It is wrong and total nonsense if you eat all essential amino acids at every meal. This is an action based on an evolutionary standpoint as our ancestors didn't examine their food choices for each meal to make sure that they were getting the right combination of proteins. They simple ate what was available. Always remember that the body recycles the required essential amino acids. So there is no point in consuming a fresh batch of each of the amino acids whether essential or not essential on a daily basis.

Gundry concludes stating that the need to revamp one's feeding habits should not be overshadowed by excuses such as:

- being already slim, fit, and active

- a need for a deep understanding of human metabolism and nutritional concepts

-Being too old to make meaningful changes in eating and other habits

CHAPTER 7: Phase 1: Kick-Start with a Three-Day Cleanse

Key Takeaways

- Cleansing the gut doesn't just repair your gut, it also repels invaders

- The source and quality of the foods you use to make your meals and snacks are critical

- A fast or cleanse changes the balance of microbes in the human system to more friendly species

A detailed explanation into the program was presented starting with the first phase which he said requires cleansing the body from all bad microbe. He maintained that this phase of cleansing and getting rid of these microbes which would be done within three days will help to restore the entire gut and other good microbes that live everywhere in and on the human body. Explaining further, in order to achieve a complete cleanse, he recommended following three important components/protocols which are:

COMPONENT 1: On and Off the Menu

He reminded the reader about the rule "what you stop eating is more important than what you start eating" which he had explained to be the defining point of the program. Gundry suggested removal of dairy, grains or pseudo-grains, fruit, sugar, seeds, eggs, soy, nightshade plants, roots, tubers, corn, soy, canola, or other inflammatory oils, along with any form of beef or other farm animal meat from the menu and replacement with dishes made with organic vegetables and small amounts of fish or pastured chicken with ingredients readily available in most well-stocked supermarkets. In addition to the foods to be included into the menu, he suggested certain snacks such as Romaine Lettuce Boats Filled with Guacamole, beverages, 8-ounces daily of protein from sources like wild-caught fish, the right condiments and seasonings such as fresh lemon juice, vinegar, fats and oils such as a whole Hass avocado each day, moderate exercise and least eight hours of sleep.

COMPONENT 2: Prepare the "Soil" and Remove the "Weeds

He recommended an optional use of Swiss Kriss which he abducted from Hauser's recommendation. He stated that the active ingredient of the herb was senna, or sennosides and that the herb can be only taken if one plans to be at home the next morning.

COMPONENT 3: Supplemental Assistance

Making reference to patients with IBS, leaky gut, or any autoimmune condition, he recommended consideration of the use of supplements to kill parasites, fungi, and other bad gut flora. These supplements include Oregon grape root extract or its active ingredient berberine, grapefruit seed extract, mushrooms or mushroom extracts, spices such as black pepper, cloves, cinnamon, and wormwood

In conclusion of the chapter, Gundry stated that carrying out a fast or cleansing process changes the balance of microbes in the body to more friendly species. He suggests the drinking more water before turning to eat more of the delicious foods available. He quickly added that getting the desired reward comes if one transitions immediately to a gut buddy.

CHAPTER 8: Phase 2: Repair and Restore

Key Takeaways

- The body has the ability to restore itself to perfect health only if you eliminate the foods and other forces that prevent it from healing.

- Not all lectins are problematic

- The legume family are the real kings of lectins and quick killers of the human immunity

- Saturated fats are not good for you: they increase hunger and appetite

Gundry discussed in a detailed process, in this chapter, how to repair and restore the body in six weeks. Reiterating the rules to observe in order to achieve success in the program, he buttressed the need to start eating foods which other diets claim to be bad. He recommended certain foods and supplements which when taken will nourish the good bacteria in the gut. These foods he explained would present as a challenge to achieve as it would replace the acclaimed healthy foods with an occurrence of withdrawal symptoms, such as low energy, headaches. To achieve an optimal restoration, he recommended the use of a list of specific foods which were to be consumed for 2 weeks out of the 6 weeks repair and restoration period.

Foods he recommended to help feed the gut include:

-resistant starches such as plantain, celery root, and Jerusalem artichokes

-raw or cooked mushrooms

-many leafy green vegetables and vegetables in the cabbage family as he claims they calm down the human system that has gone awry

-Nuts—particularly pistachios, walnuts, macadamias, and pecans

-Prebiotics that supplies fructooligosaccharides (FOS), a form of indigestible (for you) sugar that the gut requires.

-Supplements of 1000 mg per day of fish oil supplement and 5000 to 10,000 IUs as initial dose of Vitamin D.

For foods which were to be avoided, he strongly recommended removal of foods such as beans, peas, soybeans, lentils, and other members of the legume family insisting that they produced ricin, a potent lectin with high potentials of killing the human body within a minute. This reason he illustrated using the cases of food poisoning outbreaks that occurred when undercooked beans were served. For other foods, he emphasized that:

For nuts, he refuted the general belief that peanuts were nuts but insisted that it is a legume. For cashew, he explained that cashew nut is a bean and that it has the abilities to increase inflammation. Explaining further on the foods to take out, he suggested that one has to either avoid entirely these foods or apply certain methods for some of the foods if one has to indulge in it. These methods he claimed were ancient methods that were used to minimize the impact of lectins. For grains such as corn and pseudo-grain quinoa that mess with the gut wall when not properly processed he suggested the use of pressure cooker as he had observed that it destroyed these lectins.

He however, criticized the wrongly the notion of soaking dried grains as he posited that it does not remove gluten or WGA nether does sprouting legumes make them any easier to digest. These methods he explained actually increases lectin content of the foods. Still on the foods to avoid, he criticized the consumption of foods from the nightshade family such as eggplants, potatoes, peppers, goji berries, and tomatoes. However he stated that these can be consumed only when fermented as he believes it banishes the lectins in them. Continuing on the list of foods to avoid, Gundry added that:

-the squash family are to be excluded as they had very high lectin content and conveyed the store-fat-for-winter message within the body.

-the intake of fat should be limited, these fats he listed as all long-chain saturated fats, such as coconut oil and animal fats, along with most other mono- and polyunsaturated long- chain fats, such as olive oil, avocado oil. He explained that they allow the entrance of LPSs into the brain to stimulate hunger

-all out-of-season fruit should be avoided

-analgesics, stomach-acid-blocking drugs and antibiotics should be completely removed. However he recommended that for this, it is important to always check with a health-care provider before doing so.

In conclusion, he suggested the preparation of personalized diets following the rules laid out alongside the food lists but as a tip, he added that breakfast should be as light as possible, afternoon and morning snacks can be taken, salad can be eaten for lunch, while for dinner the gut should be fed with its desired meal. Citing from experience, he suggested using animal protein and salad or even resistant starch if unable to eat vegetables due to seasonal unavailability.

CHAPTER 9: Phase 3: Reap the Rewards

Key Takeaways

- You can reintroduce small amounts of lectin-containing foods into your gut.

- The safest grain is white basmati rice from India

- Moderating animal protein intake is the answer to a long, healthy life

- The myth about fasting been dangerous is wrong

- Humans can adapt to use ketones as a primary fuel

With the belief that the phases earlier mentioned has been followed, Dr Gundry listed the rewards which awaits the body when the reader is at this phase.

These awards he listed as follows:

-Absolutely change in the balance of the gut bacteria for the better.

-Almost certainly loss of three or four excess pounds, which are primarily water weight.

-Dramatic reduction of inflammation.

-An improved sense of well-being as a result of reduced inflammation

He assures that the body would achieve two things; a healed gut and that certain lectin containing foods can be reintroduced into the body. In order to introduce lectins back into the body, Gundry provided guidelines against which one could ascertain the right time to include lectins into meals again. These guidelines involve checking for signs that existed prior to starting the program.

Some of the signs he gave include:

-abnormal bowel movement

-brain fog

-painful joints

-low level of energy

-restless night and irregular sleeping pattern

-overweight or obesity

Gundry explained that this phase would become a lifestyle as he believes it would enhance one's longevity greatly. To reap the rewards of this program, Gundry outlined basic techniques that he believed would ensure that one get's a lifestyle that can be lived with. He also illuminated the tricks shared by most long-lived societies, along with the cutting-edge research that confirms these principles. His techniques are as follows:

-continuation with the food lists ensuring to avoid and eat foods as explained earlier in the provided list

-when the gut gets repaired, more ketogenic fats should be added in

-an optional reintroduction of seeded heirloom tomatoes and peppers with no skins. He advocated that based on personal tolerance one can increase the quantity consumed.

-periodic fast as he illustrated using different researches makes the body to use ketones to generate energy instead of glucose. He claimed it was the main reason behind the maintenance phase of Plant Paradox programs.

-introduction of small amounts of pressure cooked legumes

-Eating less frequent meals and less quantity of food overall

-Progressively reducing the animal protein eaten to no more than 2 ounces per day.

Following the above techniques, he assured the reader of the greatest longevity. He suggested that appropriate plants be embraced as a preferred protein source, followed probably with some small fish and rosemary. He proffered alternatives to animal protein with either intermittent fasting wherein one fasts twice a week and consequently cutting down calories to 500 to 600 a day then eating normally for the rest of the week or increasing the length of time between meals. He recommended that the gap in time between the meals should be filled up with drinking generous amounts of green tea and mint tea.

In conclusion, he recommended that in addition to the above foods and rules, the recommended supplements should be continued, there should be adequate exposure to daylight to restore daily and seasonal rhythms, blue light should be avoided, moderate exercise and getting eight hours of sleep a night are to be incorporated into one's lifestyle.

CHAPTER 10: The Keto Plant Paradox Intensive Care Program

Key Takeaways

- Eating Fat Is the Key to Unlocking Fat Storage

- Fructose, often obtained from fruits, is one of the leading causes of kidney failure

- Most diets are not kidney-sparing effect

- Intermittent fasting or stretching out the length between meals helps to boost fat burning

Dr Gundry presented this program as an alternative for patients who he called patients in dire cases such as severe diabetes, cancer, or kidney failure, or with newly diagnosed dementia or Parkinson's or other neurological diseases. He further explained that the mitochondria, energy-producing organelles of these patients' cells, were in shock due to being overlabored by the wrong foods. To explain the gradual progress of the body into the dire situation these patients were experiencing, he explained how the mitochondria functions, the effects of the over stressed and crashed mitochondria on the brain and consequently, the resulting disease states. He refuted the ideas that most diet regimens shared on the effect of consuming more protein and argued that these proteins not only created more work for the mitochondria, rather they made the brain cells to lack energy. He backed this assumptions with documented clinical findings which show that the high level of insulin in the body prevents the release of lipase an enzyme needed for ketosis.

He also suggested eating or drinking ketones made from plants as seen in Medium-chain triglycerides (MCT oil) Examples he provided includes solid coconut oil, palm fruit oil. Again he repeated his recommendations that these types of patients should remove animal protein entirely from their meal plan as taking in these ketones will not be effective if there is excessive protein in the body. Referring to a clinical research, he explained that insulin facilitates fat conversion to ketones and without the removal of these animal protein which are in excess, even with continuous intake of ketones the patient would never achieve ketosis, a point everyone has been made to know promotes weight loss.

In continuation, Dr Gundry examined the relationship between cancer, diabetes and kidney failure and ketones. Based on researches carried out on cancer, he concluded that cancer cell mitochondria, unlike the normal cell mitochondria, can only obtain energy using these two mechanisms:

-relying on the extremely inefficient system of sugar fermentation also used by yeasts and bacteria,

-fermenting sugar in the form of fructose rather than glucose.

He added that protein, carbs, and fruit are the real enemies while fat and ketones are the right friends for the gut. He assured the users of the program that the kidney would be spared as it would turn the body to start break down of ketone for energy instead of waiting for insulin. He recommended the practice of intermittent fasting as he believes that it helps to burn fat faster given both personal and patients' experience. He added that if the patient was not eating, he recommended supplementing the body every few hours with a tablespoon of MCT oil or coconut oil; to avoid brain fog, weakness, or being dizzy.

As he had done for the basic paradox, he listed out foods to eat and foods to avoid or taken in limited quantity. Foods to eat includes the same as in the basic plant paradox, while for foods to avoid he insisted that all fruits be avoided except those that are listed as resistant starches such as avocados, green bananas and plantains, green mangos, and green papayas. Inclusive into the list, he requested that patients with cancer should try to eliminate animal proteins altogether. His reason given that these proteins contain a greater concentration of the amino acids that cancer cells use than do plant sources of protein. Rather, he recommended the consumption of leaves, tubers, and root vegetables as they would provide all the protein their bodies needed but the cancer calls cannot use.

In conclusion, he cleared the air on how long the Keto Plant Paradox Intensive Care Program should be followed. He explained there was no need to rush it, rather that it should be regarded as a program as a path to a lifestyle one can live with, a lifestyle which he assure would be life- and health-affirming.

CHAPTER 11: Plant Paradox Supplement Recommendations

Key Takeaways

- Proper diet and certain supplements are key components of what will become your gut protection and repair strategy

- Supplements enhance the results of the this program but they are not substitutes for the program

- Foods—fruits, vegetables and grains-no longer contain enough of certain needed nutrients

- Plants are both our bane and our salvation

Dr Gundry stated that there is not enough natural nutrients available in soil for plant use and as such, he concludes that even grasses do not have enough to get from the soil. With this observation, he highlights use of supplements as a critical component of the Plant Paradox Program. He lists supplements that should be replenished with recommendations of various sources and doses to use.

-For Vitamin D3, he suggests that starters should use just 5000 IUs of vitamin D3 daily. For autoimmune disease, 10,000IUs a day. He reassures of no toxicity recorded with these doses.

-For B Vitamins, he emphasizes that Methylfolate and Methylcobalamin be taken especially as they are gut vitamins. He emphasized the two particular vitamins as important due to being able to turn amino acids from breakdown of protein into a harmless substance in the body. He suggests swallowing a methylfolate 1000 mcg tablet each day and putting a 1000 to 5000 mcg methyl B12 under the tongue. He pointed out that this method of ingestion bypasses genetic mutation.

To complete the lists of supplements he recommends, he listed six most important classes of supplements which he called the G6. They include:

Polyphenols: He helps us understand that these are compounds are used by the plant to resist insects and protect against sunburn. He states that they block the formation of the atherosclerosis-causing trimethylamine N-oxide (TMAO) from the animal proteins carnitine and choline preventing the process of atherosclerosis form starting and at the same time, provides a host of beneficial effects when metabolized by the gut bacteria. For the doses, he suggested 100 mg of both grape seed extract and resveratrol, and 25 to 100 mg of pine tree bark extract a day.

Green Plant Phytochemicals: Using his medical experience, he proves that these supplements tend to suppress appetite for the bad stuff that makes one fat. Suggesting come supplements, he recommends spinach extract available in

500 mg capsules to be taken two per day, DIM available in capsule form to be taken 100 mg a day and modified citrus pectin available as a powder or in 500 mg capsules to be taken two capsules or one scoop per day.

Prebiotics: He noted that some compounds are used for the treatment of constipation, such as psyllium powder or husks, are not only bowel stimulator laxatives, but can serve as food for the gut microbes. This he concludes makes them grow and multiply, accounting for that bigger bowel movement. He persuades that one should feed the good guys and starve the bad guys rather. He recommended starting with a teaspoon of psyllium powder a day in water and thereafter, work up to a tablespoon a day, then followed by adding a teaspoon of inulin powder a day.

Lectin Blockers: He admits that at some point, one might mistakenly consume lectins. In order to prevent any issues from coming up, he suggests the use of a number of helpful lectin-absorbing compounds on the market, take glucosamine and MSM available in tablet form.

Sugar Defense

With the effect of sugars in the body, he states the need to be on the defensive side against these killers. He recommended CinSulin, which combines chromium and cinnamon to be taken two capsules a day, combined with 30 mg of zinc once a day, 150 mcg of selenium a day, 250 mg of berberine twice a day, and 200 mg of turmeric extract twice a day.

Long-Chain Omega-3s

Having proved the good effects of these supplements, he suggests choosing a fish oil that is molecularly distilled and comes from small fish such as sardines and anchovies.

With these suggestions made, Dr Gundry assures the reader of a better health and well being only on the basis that this program was followed to the letter.

Review And Analysis Of Plant Paradox

This book provides information and research based facts on the myths surrounding food and how it affects the body. According to Dr. Steven Gundry, He claims that the so called "health foods" are to be blamed For Causing Sickness and Over Weight in Today's World. In This book, it's expects that the reader knows that the effects of weight and other related food problems are as a result of the plant based foods and fruits consumed over the years. The Plant Paradox Book, explains that plants actually want to make the human body ill by destroying the body in order to survive and reproduce its offspring to continue their existence in the world. The evidence based research showing that despite the fact that plants are evolving, humans are not doing same at the same rate as these plants and other mammals and as such; are prone to becoming easily affected by the killing effects of plants. In addition to this, these plants being consumed are not rightly cooked or are poorly cooked making the body digestion to be more prone to the toxicity of these plants. Researches from well known scientists have shown the effects of these plants by extracting their toxins to test on lower animals and from the study of diseased humans. Dr. Gundry argues that other diets prior to this have all been getting it all wrong as they do not work in line with various researches and laid down facts on the harmful effects of consuming this plant based diets. The book aims to persuade its users that there are ways food can be used to make the body whole again from diseases which affect it, ways to eat these foods that contain the toxicity with the help of special cooking instruments and that the body can return to its state only if these processes and stated phases of life changing activities are followed. The claims and suggested guides were presented in detailed and step by step process and were backed with evidence from research, personal experience and treatments observed in patients. Most of these assumptions have been documented in various research articles and publications and were presented using a clear format and examples from case studies seen in patients to show that this regimen for treatment of diseases works.

Furthermore, the book recommends that in order for one to feel healthier and live a better and long life, one has to start with eliminating overreliance on certain foods as a primary form of sustenance. It brings together the different types of foods based on its seed type to state the right ones to eat to become healthier and the ones to add or up its consumption in order to live a long and fruitful life at the end.

Ultimate List of Lectin Free foods to Replace For a Healthy Weight Loss

Replace This...   **With This!**

Fine table salt............................. Fine Sea Salt

Kosher salt .... Iodized Sea salt

Canola Oil .... Avocado Oil

Vegetable Oil .... Extra-virgin olive oil

Popcorn .... Popped Sorghum

Commercial Chicken, beef broth .... Vegetable, mushroom broth

Sesame oil blend ....Toasted sesame oil

Canned Tuna .... Canned wild salmon

Brown rice .... Indian Basmatic Rice

Agave Syrup .... Yacon Syrup

Filtered, pasteurized honey....... Local Raw Honey

Crackers .... Flax seed Crackers

Breakfast Cereal .... Puffed millet

Peanut Butter .... White Almond Butter

Crackers .... Flax seed Crackers

Rice noodles .... Shirataki noodles

Corn/ flour Tortillas …………………….. Almond Flour Tortillas

Chips, pretzel ……………………….. Great Plantain Chip

Whole Wheat Flour …………………. Tigernut Flour

All-Purpose Flour ……………………. Cassava Flour

Imitation Vanilla ……………………… Pure Vanilla Extract

Semi-sweet baking Chocolate…… Dark Chocolate (75% or more)

Bread Crumbs ……………………………… Groundnuts

Evaporated milk ………………………. Full Fat Coconut Milk

Mayo …………………………………………. Avocado Mayo

Hummus………………………………….Tahini

Dried Fruit; Cranberries, cherries, raisins … Dried Figs (unsweetened)

Peanuts, cashews …………………. Macadamia nuts, pistachios

Powdered sugar …………………….. Powdered Erythritol

Maple Syrup …………………………. Erythritol Syrup

Granulated sugar ……………….. Granulated Erythritol

Soy sauce, tamari ………………. Coconut Aminos

Dried, Canned Beans …………. Eden Brand Beans

Sesame Oil Blend .... Toasted Sesame Oil

Thanks So Much For The Support. If you Enjoyed This

Summary of The Plant Paradox

Take a Little Time to Leave Us A Review.

It will be well appreciated!

One or Two Statement Will Go a Long Way in

Helping Other People Looking to Buy.

Made in the USA
Lexington, KY
16 August 2018